I'm a Little Teapot

I'm a Little Teapot

As told and illustrated by

Iza Trapani

Gareth Stevens Publishing
MILWAUKEE

A special "thank you" to Emma, Max, and Mick
for their wonderful suggestions.

For a free color catalog describing Gareth Stevens' list of high-quality books
and multimedia programs, call 1-800-542-2595 (USA) or 1-800-461-9120 (Canada).
Gareth Stevens Publishing's Fax: (414) 225-0377

Library of Congress Cataloging-in-Publication Data

Trapani, Iza.
I'm a little teapot / as told and illustrated by Iza Trapani.
p. cm. — (Extended nursery rhymes)
Summary: Expanded verses of a familiar song tell how a teapot dreams
of visiting China, Mexico, the opera, a jungle, and other places while waiting
to be used to serve tea. Includes music and lyrics on the last page.
ISBN 0-8368-2487-3 (lib. bdg.)
1. Children's songs—Texts. [1. Teapots—Songs and music.
2. Imagination—Songs and music. 3. Songs.] I. Title. II. Series.
PZ8.3.T686Iae 1999
782.42164'0268—dc21
[E]   99-25775

This edition first published in 1999 by
Gareth Stevens Publishing
1555 North RiverCenter Drive, Suite 201
Milwaukee, WI 53212 USA

Original edition published by Whispering Coyote Press, Inc.,
300 Crescent Court, Suite 860, Dallas, TX 75201.
Original book and illustrations © 1996 by Whispering Coyote Press, L.P.

Printed in the United States of America

1 2 3 4 5 6 7 8 9 03 02 01 00 99

For Jeannie, Laura, and Teri,
"friends forever!"
Love,
Iza

I'm a little teapot, short and stout.
Here is my handle, here is my spout.
When I get all steamed up, hear me shout,
Just tip me over, pour me out!

I'm a little teapot, come see me.
Oh how I'd love your company.
Sitting on the stove top patiently,
I wait for someone to make tea.

9

I'm a little teapot, I'll show you
All of the things that I'd like to do.
It's a game I play the whole day through.
Now let me share my dreams with you.

I'm a little teapot, on that note
We're off to China—grab your coat.
We can fly a kite and row our boat
And eat with chopsticks as we float.

13

I'm a little teapot, si señor.
All over Mexico we can tour.
I'll become a mighty matador
And fight the bull while you keep score.

I'm a little teapot, watch me fly
Just like a spaceship in the sky.
On another planet way up high,
We'll meet an alien eye to eye.

16

I'm a little teapot, la, la, la!
Let's take a trip to the opera.
You can sing a lovely aria,
And I'll play in the orchestra.

I'm a little teapot, hey let's play
Pirates at sea on a windy day.
Back and forth our sailing ship will sway.
Ahoy my mateys! Find the way!

21

I'm a little teapot, tally ho!
Off on a fox hunt we will go.
Racing with the hounds, our trumpets blow.
Now where on earth did that fox go?

23

I'm a little teapot, peekaboo!
Deep in the jungle I'll hide with you.
You can try to find me, if you do—
Then you can hide and I'll find you.

I'm a little teapot, golly gee!
Thank you for sharing my dreams with me.
Now I'd really like to make some tea
For all your friends and family.

I'm a little teapot, short and stout.
Here is my handle, here is my spout.
Tip me over gently, pour me out
For that's what tea time's all about!

31

I'm a Little Teapot

I'm a lit-tle tea-pot, short and stout. Here is my han-dle,

here is my spout. When I get all steamed up,

hear me shout. Just tip me ov-er, and pour me out!

1. I'm a little teapot, short and stout.
Here is my handle, here is my spout.
When I get all steamed up, hear me shout.
Just tip me over, pour me out!

2. I'm a little teapot, come see me.
Oh how I'd love your company.
Sitting on the stove top patiently,
I wait for someone to make tea.

3. I'm a little teapot, I'll show you
All of the things that I'd like to do.
It's a game I play the whole day through.
Now let me share my dreams with you.

4. I'm a little teapot, on that note
We're off to China—grab your coat.
We can fly a kite and row our boat
And eat with chopsticks as we float.

5. I'm a little teapot, si señor.
All over Mexico we can tour.
I'll become a mighty matador
And fight the bull while you keep score.

6. I'm a little teapot, watch me fly
Just like a spaceship in the sky.
On another planet way up high,
We'll meet an alien eye to eye.

7. I'm a little teapot, la, la, la!
Let's take a trip to the opera.
You can sing a lovely aria,
And I'll play in the orchestra.

8. I'm a little teapot, hey let's play
Pirates at sea on a windy day.
Back and forth our sailing ship will sway.
Ahoy my mateys! Find the way!

9. I'm a little teapot, tally ho!
Off on a fox hunt we will go.
Racing with the hounds, our trumpets blow.
Now where on earth did that fox go?

10. I'm a little teapot, peekaboo!
Deep in the jungle I'll hide with you.
You can try to find me, if you do—
Then you can hide and I'll find you.

11. I'm a little teapot, golly gee!
Thank you for sharing my dreams with me.
Now I'd really like to make some tea
For all your friends and family.

12. I'm a little teapot, short and stout.
Here is my handle, here is my spout.
Tip me over gently, pour me out
For that's what tea time's all about!